CONTENTS

INTRODUCTION TO ATHEISM

On September 14, 1998, John Paul II released *Fides et Ratio* (*Faith and Reason*). In this encyclical, the Holy Father stresses the need for sound philosophy.[1] Good philosophy enables us to understand our faith more deeply and to recognize contemporary errors more clearly. It also enables us to find true answers to the problems of human existence.

In his encyclical, as well as in his book *Crossing the Threshold of Hope*, John Paul II traces many serious errors of our day to bad philosophy. He points out that many false ideologies, such as rationalism and atheism, originated from the philosophical errors of the period known as the Enlightenment. The Holy Father wants us to understand the foundations of these errors so that we can identify and refute them in whatever form they appear.

Several weeks after releasing *Faith and Reason*, John Paul II emphasized that sound

> *The Church ... sees in philosophy the way to come to know fundamental truths about human life. At the same time, the Church considers philosophy an indispensable help for a deeper understanding of faith and for communicating the truth of the Gospel to those who do not yet know it.*
>
> Faith and Reason, 5

philosophy must be taught to all Catholic laymen, not just seminarians and theology students. He wants the average Catholic to have at least a beginner's grasp of current philosophical errors.

In order to help carry out the wishes of the Holy Father, we have compiled this booklet for those Catholics who don't have an extensive background in philosophy. We focus on the many ways that atheism is promoted today as well as on the false philosophies used to defend it. We devote a lot of attention to the French Enlightenment, which John Paul II identifies as the source for many of the present atheistic ideologies.

Before we deal with the Enlightenment, we first discuss the pursuit of truth, errors in that pursuit, and proofs for the existence of God. We then examine some early modern philosophies that paved the way for the Enlightenment, then the Enlightenment itself and the many atheistic systems it spawned. Finally, we will consider the "New Atheists" who are promoting atheism in our own day.

We hope this booklet will give Catholics a good overview of the philosophical origins of modern atheism as well as the tools to expose and refute them.

---

1 Philosophy (from the Greek philos + sophia: "loving wisdom") means the pursuit of foundational or ultimate truths using the light of human reason.

FINDING THE TRUTH

We live in an age of widespread atheism. College students are often exposed to atheism under the guise of science and philosophy. Sometimes they are told outright that an educated person no longer needs the "crutch" of religion. In the last century, billions of people lived under regimes where atheism was the state religion. Elsewhere, socialist parties governed with a totally atheistic mentality, even if they didn't write it into their constitutions.

However, atheism as a philosophy or political system is relatively new. In past ages, the occasional person who didn't believe in a divine power was considered an oddball and a frivolous thinker. Why has the modern age produced so many atheistic ideologies? What philosophies of the early modern age (1500–1700) planted the seeds of the atheistic systems of the last two centuries?

Before we begin to study modern atheism and the many disguised ways it is promoted today, it will be helpful to examine some preliminary topics that will give us the tools to critique modern atheism:

① The Pursuit of Truth and Belief in God;

② Why the Search for Truth Can Go Astray;

③ Proofs for the Existence of God.

THE PURSUIT OF TRUTH AND BELIEF IN GOD

Among all creatures in the visible world, only human beings are made in the image and likeness of God. Because we are made in God's image, we have spiritual souls that enable us to know and contemplate truth. The power of the soul that can know is called the intellect. The intellect's object or goal is truth.

The intellect was made for truth. Even ancient thinkers recognized that man naturally seeks truth. Man is never satisfied in his quest for truth and understanding. God gave man this power to know and understand truth so that he would seek  and find the ultimate Truth: God Himself. As St. Augustine observed, "You have made us for Yourself, O Lord, and our hearts are restless until they rest in You."

God reveals Himself to human beings in three ways. He does this through:

① **The Material Universe**. The material universe is the artwork of God, the Divine Artist. Just as we can learn a lot about an artist by studying his paintings, so we can learn a lot about God by studying His universe.

② **The Natural Moral Law**. This law is written in our hearts. With our God-given reason, we can recognize the demands of the eternal moral law. Many people call this the "voice of conscience," in which God speaks directly to our hearts.

③ **Public Revelation**. This includes both Sacred Scripture and Sacred Tradition.

Obviously, those who haven't received the benefit of public revelation, or who refuse to accept it, have only the created material universe and the natural moral law to guide them. However, by examining the universe and the demands of the natural law, any reasonable person is able to know God's existence and power. Therefore, as St. Paul tells us in Romans, even pagans have no excuse for denying God's existence:

> **Romans 1:19-20:** For what can be known about God is plain to them, because God has shown it to them. Ever since the creation of the world his invisible nature, namely, his eternal power and deity, *has been clearly perceived in the things that have been made.* So they are without excuse.

But didn't original sin do irreparable damage to the human intellect? It's true that because of original sin, man's intellect has been wounded and often causes him to err in his pursuit of truth. But even with a darkened intellect, man retains great power for arriving at truth. This is why St. Paul held the pagans accountable for denying God.

WHY THE SEARCH FOR TRUTH CAN GO ASTRAY

In order to understand why people go astray in their search for God, we must look at the different ways people can err in their pursuit of truth. We have already mentioned the *intellect* was darkened by original sin. The effects of original sin also darkened the other faculty of the soul, the *will*. The will has the power to choose, and therefore to love. Just as the intellect naturally seeks the *truth*, the will naturally seeks the *good*.

Obviously, the intellect can sometimes fail to grasp the truth. Even if the intellect does attain the truth, often the will, because of its weakness, chooses a false or lesser good instead of the true good. The intellect and will can each mislead the other. If the will is attracted to evil, the intellect can distort the truth to make the evil seem more acceptable. If the intellect mistakes something evil for something good, the will naturally chooses the apparent good (the evil) rather than the true good.

We should keep these points in mind as we examine some of the reasons why the pursuit of truth often goes astray.

Faulty Foundations

➤ **Imagination.** We can substitute imagination in place of facts and sound reasoning. For example, the gods of Greek mythology were completely products of the imagination. Yet many people worshipped them as if they really existed. Other people regard their dreams as real, and act accordingly. The imagination is a good thing. It can be extremely useful for creativity and meditation. Still, because of original  sin, the imagination is an unreliable guide to truth. It should never be a substitute for facts and sound reasoning in the search for truth.

➤ **Emotions.** We can rely on emotions instead of evidence and clear thinking. Like imagination, emotions are valuable. They often provide the energy and motivation to pursue truth and goodness. Nevertheless, like the imagination, emotions have been wounded by original sin and are thus extremely untrustworthy guides to the truth. We should never substitute emotions for clear thinking. Reason has also been affected by original sin, but not as extensively as imagination and emotion. Reason is generally still a reliable guide to the truth, whereas imagination and emotion are not. When we believe something because we "feel" it's true, or when we believe people because we like their physical appearance or political party, we are using emotion instead of reason and facts. Those who say "listen to your heart" instead of to your head are simply wrong.

➤ **Moral Error.** We can be seduced by moral error. Pride and immorality can blind us to the facts. This is more a problem of the will than the intellect. Often, people don't seek the truth sincerely because it contradicts their immoral lifestyle or wounds their swollen pride. They deliberately fail to examine all the evidence that points to the true God. They ignore miracles and the many compelling arguments for God's existence. They know the God of public revelation makes strict moral demands. Accepting and obeying God will require radical lifestyle changes. Their pride also keeps them from accepting the existence— even worse, the *authority*—of a being infinitely more powerful and intelligent than they are. Pride and immorality are perhaps the most common reasons why people reject God's existence.

Faulty Reasoning

Faulty reasoning is another frequent cause of people straying in their pursuit of truth.

The following are some widespread types of incorrect thinking:

➤ Failing to identify the *inconsistencies and contradictions* in the evidence and arguments that we encounter. People are rarely educated today about principles of sound reasoning or how to detect logical fallacies. Consequently, they have little ability to distinguish false arguments from true ones.

➤ Failing to see that the *conclusions presented don't follow from the given facts*. Many times the similarities between the evidence and the conclusion are only superficial, apparent, or irrelevant. This is a fault common to those who promote atheism. Atheistic Darwinian evolutionists commit this error repeatedly.

Charles Darwin

➤ Failing to identify *ambiguous and misleading statements*. The key to catching this error is to carefully examine the key words in an argument: is their meaning being shifted or redefined? Lack of precision and clarity in the use of words is an indication that a person either doesn't know his material well or is deliberately trying to mislead.

➤ Failing to identify *assertions that are totally unconnected* to the issue at hand. Many times people will pile up irrelevant assertions to stall, confuse, or mislead. A person's unwillingness to stay focused is often a sign that his argument is weak or false.

➤ Failing to recognize *misplaced authority*. We often assume that an expert in one

Carl Sagan

field must be an expert in a completely unrelated field. For example, many people accept Carl Sagan's atheistic views because he was a great astronomer. They fail to recognize that being an expert astronomer didn't necessarily make him an expert theologian. In fact, his arguments against God's existence are quite superficial. Again, many people accept abortion simply because some doctors support it. They fail to see that a well-trained doctor might have a poor knowledge of basic moral principles.

➤ Failing to recognize that *experts in their fields aren't always objective*. Scientists, doctors, and philosophers often have prejudices and preconceptions that can bias their research and conclusions.

Many fallacies and contradictions are difficult to detect because they are buried in a mass of complicated, technical details. This is why errors promoted by well-known philosophers and scientists often go unchallenged. They tend to formulate their ideas in long and complicated books. It takes great patience to carefully dissect and analyze their arguments.

These are some of the major causes why people go astray in their quest for truth. These failures are also clear evidence that our intellects have been darkened by original sin and are prone to error. If the intellect goes astray in identifying what is truly good, the will chooses lesser goods, or even false goods. This is why history is filled with cultures that worshipped false gods and embraced depraved moral practices.

PROOFS FOR THE EXISTENCE OF GOD

Through the use of human reason alone, man can know that God exists:

> Our holy mother, the Church, holds and teaches that God, the first principle and last end of all things, can be known with certainty from the created world by the natural light of human reason.[2]

Not only does reason tell us that God exists, it also reveals many important things about God: that He is one, spiritual, eternal, and uncreated. Some truths about God cannot be known by human reason alone, such as the Trinity and the Incarnation. These mysteries can only be known by public revelation.

How can reason tell us that God exists? There are five classic proofs for the existence of God. St. Thomas Aquinas lists them in the *Summa Theologiae*:

① The need for a **Prime Mover**.

② The need for a **First Cause**.

③ The need for a **Necessary Being**.

④ The need for a **Supremely Perfect Being**.

⑤ The need for an **Intelligent Designer**.

Proofs 1, 3, and 4 are highly philosophical and thus, not ideal to use with an atheist. Atheists tend to be steeped in materialism and attached to the scientific method. They are not ordinarily moved by abstract arguments. Arguments that resemble those used in science and that rely

2 *Catechism of the Catholic Church* 36.

heavily on the observable universe will be more convincing to an atheist. Proofs 2 and 5 are best suited for this. These arguments are also easier to understand and strongly supported by recent scientific discoveries.

The Need for a First Cause

Everyone with the use of reason can easily grasp that everything in the material universe is explained by a previous cause. Nothing begins to exist without a cause. Nothing can cause its own existence. Every material object is the end product of a long chain of causes. If we go back far enough, we end up asking the ultimate questions: why does matter exist at all? Where does it come from?

Just like every other material object in the universe, matter itself needs a previous cause to explain its existence. Since nothing can cause itself,[3] why does matter exist? The only answer is that some power outside the material universe created matter to begin with. That power must be *spirit*, because it is outside the material universe. That power must be *infinite* to create something out of absolutely nothing. The gap between nothing and something, between non-being and actual existence, is infinite. It takes an infinite power to bridge that infinite gap. Only God has infinite power.

Recent discoveries in astrophysics have proven scientifically that the universe had a clear beginning: the Big Bang. This makes the First Cause proof especially compelling to atheists. Simply ask: "Who set off the Big Bang?" Many astrophysicists who are on the cutting edge of recent discoveries are answering, "God."

The Need for an Intelligent Designer

When we see a complicated system that has been perfectly constructed for a obvious purpose, common sense tells us that an intelligent being is responsible. For example, if we found a perfectly running watch in the middle of the wilderness, we wouldn't even consider that this watch came into existence by chance. Why? For two important reasons:

---

3 Nothing in the universe has ever been observed to cause its own existence, to make itself exist when it didn't exist before. Nothing just "pops" itself into existence.

Would the argument change if matter *always* existed? No. Matter would still need a cause to explain its existence. Remember, nothing can make itself, nothing can give itself existence. Even if matter were eternal, there would have to be a co-eternal, infinite power that caused matter to exist. This co-eternal power wouldn't be prior in time, but would be prior in *causality*, since it gave matter its eternal existence. At this point the skeptic usually asks: "If nothing can make itself, then who made God?" The answer is, of course, no one made God. God always existed. He alone is the First Cause, the Uncaused Cause on which all other causes depend. We can't have an infinite series of causes without eventually arriving at the First Cause, the cause with no prior cause. We can't have an infinitely tall building without a bottom floor, or an infinitely long train of moving railroad cars without an engine. Eventually we must come to the independent thing on which all the other things depend, the hook on which the whole chain of causes hangs. Everything else depends on the First Cause, but the First Cause doesn't depend on anything. It simply *is* and always was.

① The object is composed of many complicated, perfectly arranged parts.

② The object was designed for a clear purpose: to tell time.

We immediately know there must have been intelligent beings responsible for the watch. No atheist would argue with this obvious conclusion.

Consider the human eye. It is an amazingly complicated organ that is arranged for a clear purpose: to see. The development of the eye from the first cells in the embryo to the fully mature organ consists of countless steps in which many complex elements come together in perfect harmony. Each complex step in the process could only proceed because a previous complex step occurred correctly. The chain of steps is extremely long, as any microbiologist will confirm. This long, intricate process proceeds toward a clear purpose: to form an organ capable of sight.

Assembling a watch is relatively easy. But no one argues that watches are made by chance. Assembling an eye is unbelievably complicated. All the scientists of the world working together with the most advanced technology cannot synthesize a human eye. Yet, atheists insist the development of the human eye is the result of purely random, chaotic processes. The marvel of the human eye virtually screams: "intelligent design!" Intelligent design demands an intelligent designer.

If we examine the material world, we find countless examples of complex, purposeful systems that require an intelligent designer. In living organisms, we could look at the brain, the heart, the ears, or the digestive system. In the nonliving world, we can look at the findings of modern astronomy. With amazing tools like the Hubble telescope, we are discovering that the universe is more complicated than we ever dreamed. At the same time, it is more perfectly organized than we ever suspected.

Astrophysicists have shown that the universe began with "the Big Bang," an explosion so powerful that it staggers the imagination. This awesome blast had to be regulated within an extremely narrow range in order for the universe to be formed. If the speed of the elements in the explosion had moved just fractionally faster or slower, there would have been only chaos instead of the amazingly complex, perfectly organized universe we know. Scientists tell us that events appeared to have been "guided" to bring about a planet like earth, capable of sustaining intelligent life.[4]

Amazingly, the bodies and movements of the universe appear to have been "deliberately" made to correspond to the operations of the human mind and to be intelligible to it. Like the human eye, the processes of the material universe seem to shout: "intelligent design!" Given

---

4 We recommend Hugh Ross's excellent book, *The Creator and the Cosmos: How the Greatest Scientific Discoveries of the Century Reveal God* (Colorado Springs, CO: NavPress, 1995). Ross explains how recent scientific measurements of the universe clearly point to God's existence. Also see his *Why the Universe Is the Way It Is* (Grand Rapids, MI: Baker Books, 2008).

the immense size and complexity of the universe, it is easy to see that this intelligent designer must be God.

We can go even further and say the awesome power, order, beauty, and majesty of the universe appear designed to reflect the infinite power, order, beauty, and majesty of God.

Miracles

Atheists deny miracles. They realize accepting miracles means accepting God. A miracle is an event or act that is beyond the ability of any natural power. A miracle is, by definition, supernatural. We have many authenticated miracles including incorrupt saints, instantaneous healings, Eucharistic miracles, and miraculous images. There are also inexplicable events such as the dancing sun at Fatima and the liquefaction of the blood of St. Januarius (a miracle that occurs several times every year).

St. Bernadette

Many of these miracles (such as incorrupt saints and Eucharistic marvels) are still visible to the public. They are verifiable for anyone with eyes to see and the ability to travel. We should invite atheists to examine

Eucharistic Miracle at Lanciano

these public miracles firsthand and to go where the evidence leads them.

The Spirituality of the Human Soul

Proving the spirituality of the human soul accomplishes two important things:

① it proves the existence of the spiritual—thus refuting materialism, the claim that only material things exist; and

② it proves the need for direct creation of the soul out of nothing, since a spiritual substance has no parts and thus can't come into being through generation.

If we can show direct creation out of nothing, as demonstrated earlier, we have proved the existence of an infinitely powerful Being.

Proving the spirituality or immateriality of the human soul is easy. Human beings can study the visible world and, from sensible experiences of material objects or events, create purely immaterial realities called *ideas*. For example, a person sees crimes being committed and criminals being punished. From these observations the mind forms the idea of "justice," a purely spiritual reality. He may see justice being applied in individual cases, but the idea of "justice" is a universal, abstract concept that is immaterial or spiritual.[5]

---

5 If you doubt this, simply form any abstract idea in your mind and ask yourself: "How much does this idea weigh? How long is it? What color is it? What shape is it? How much space does it take up?" The answer is that your idea has no weight, no length, no color, no shape, and takes up no space. It simply has no material attributes at all. Something with *no material* attributes is *immaterial*, another word for spiritual. This and other arguments are found in F. J. Sheed's highly-recommended book, *Theology for Beginners* (Ann Arbor, MI: Servant Books, 1981), 9–16.

Immaterial *ideas* imply an immaterial *faculty* capable of forming them. It is impossible for something material to create something immaterial. Therefore, the faculty capable of forming spiritual ideas must itself be spiritual. This spiritual faculty can only come from a spiritual substance, the soul.

---

*In short,
human thinking reveals the ability
to form purely immaterial concepts,
called* ideas.

*These immaterial concepts require
an immaterial faculty,
the* intellect.

*This immaterial faculty requires a
spiritual reality, the* soul.

The Problem of Evil or Suffering

Atheists often point to the existence of evil and suffering in the world as proof that God doesn't exist. Their argument goes something like this: "If there really were an all-good, all-knowing, all-powerful God, there wouldn't be evil in the world."[6] Evil and suffering can pose great difficulties even for believers, especially on an emotional level. But the problem of evil poses greater difficulties for atheists.

---

6 This argument cuts both ways. If evil *disproves* God's existence, then good (which we assume when we call something else evil) *proves* God's existence. If we account for evil by denying God, then we are left with an even larger problem: how do we account for the obvious good in the world?

Consider the following observations:

➤ Evil and suffering in the world don't affect the compelling proofs for the existence of God.

➤ If an atheist comes to believe in God, he will learn that God has given man a marvelous gift: free will. Man's abuse of free will has brought much suffering and evil into the world. It's not God's fault we have misused His gift.

➤ Suffering can be beneficial. Many times suffering causes people to grow in character. There's a Jewish adage, "The man who has not suffered, what can he possibly know?" On the other hand, some suffering, especially the suffering of innocents such as infants, raises difficulties that we cannot pretend to answer.

In summary, when atheists bring up the problem of evil and suffering in the world, we should tell them:

➤ The problem of evil doesn't let you off the hook. You must still face the proofs for the existence of God.

➤ Through public revelation, believers have an explanation for a great deal of the suffering and evil in the world. We also have the certainty that we will get all the answers at the Last Judgement.

➤ You atheists face the same suffering and evil as the believer. The difference is that you have *no answers* and *no hope* of ever finding any.

THE ROOTS OF MODERN ATHEISM

Before we examine the roots of modern atheism, we should note some of the important movements of the early modern age (1500–1700).

➤ **Scientific Method**. The scientific method of study profoundly affected modern man's view of the world. Many of the leading thinkers of the time began to look down on other ways of pursuing the truth. They regarded philosophical and theological methods as unreliable. Since philosophy and theology are the only ways to examine spiritual realities, the result was a tendency to ignore spiritual realities or to study them with the wrong approach.

➤ **Individualism and Subjectivism**. The rise of rugged individualism and subjectivism led to a contempt or rejection of traditional authority figures. This mentality is seen, for example, in the private interpretation of the Bible among Protestants who tended to regard Church guidance in this area as completely unnecessary.

➤ **Ancient Paganism**. Renewed interest in antiquity revived pagan ideas, many of them good. Unfortunately, pagan ideas about immorality tended to be the most popular. Their popularity fueled the desire of many people to abandon strict Christian moral teachings. Much of the rebellion against Christianity was the result of revived pagan immorality.

➤ **Secular Achievements**. The modern nation-state, the great exploration movements, and improvements in living conditions unfortunately led many people to turn their attention away from God and the afterlife and to focus instead on purely earthly rewards.

We will now look at some of the major philosophies of the early modern age that prepared the way for the atheistic philosophies of the last two centuries.

DEISM

Generally traced to the English thinker, **Edward Herbert** (1582–1648), deism is a stripped-down version of Christianity. It  was a religion without doctrines, without churches, and without public revelation. Deism did retain a belief in a Supreme Being, right and wrong, and afterlife rewards or punishments.

A later view of deism viewed God as a kind of "Divine Watchmaker." God was the Supreme Being who designed the universe and then left it to its own devices. According to this view, after creating the universe, God ceased to care for it.

Some forms of deism view God as a "Divine Watchmaker" who designed the universe and then left it to run by itself.

This later view of deism is important to know because it was the religion of the

12

Enlightenment (see page 16). This was an 18th-century intellectual movement that questioned traditional religious beliefs and stressed the primacy of reason and the strict scientific method. The Enlightenment spawned the major atheistic systems of the last two centuries.

Deism provided a "respectable" transition between the traditional Christianity of Europe and later modern atheism. It would have been nearly impossible for atheism to gain a large following in 16th- and 17th-century Europe. However, early deism—which believed in right and wrong, a Supreme Being, and an afterlife—quickly gained a following among the scholars of the 17th century. Once many educated people had accepted early deism, it became easy for them accept later deism's concept of a remote, uninvolved, and unknowable God. Once God is viewed as distant, indifferent to human affairs, and totally incomprehensible, the step to outright atheism is a short one.

The god of later deism was appealing to men steeped in the scientific method. God was the "divine scientist" who made this marvelous machine we call the universe and then moved on. Just as the ancient pagans projected their pagan mindset into their ideas of God, so too did many early modern thinkers project their scientific mindset into their concept of God.

IDEALISM

The dominant philosophy of 17th-century Europe was known as idealism. It has had a profound impact on modern thought since that time. It greatly influenced the development of the 18th-century Enlightenment.

We must distinguish between idealism as a philosophy (a bad thing) and the common meaning of idealism: having lofty goals, standards, and objectives (a good thing). The philosophy of idealism took many forms, some of them quite complicated. However, because of its important connection to atheistic philosophies, we should at least be aware of some of its major themes.

Idealism taught the following:

➤ *A radical separation between the mind and the external world.* It was almost as if the mind belonged to a completely different realm.

➤ *A radical split between a person's mind and his body.* It is the mind alone that makes the person. The body, being material, isn't important. The mind only "uses" the body.

Comment: We can see how this belief would draw people away from the Incarnation. It also undermines the suffering, death, and resurrection of Jesus. If the body is not important, these mysteries lose their meaning and significance. This radical separation between mind and body goes  back to ancient paganism (Platonism). It is closely linked to the doctrine of reincarnation, where the same soul uses a different body in each new life.

➤ *That the world outside of us can't be known with any certainty.* The information gained through the senses can't be trusted.

Comment: Idealists had an extremely negative view of the senses. They considered them totally unreliable. Since our five senses put us in contact with the material world, we can see why idealists considered  the material world to be unknowable. As we have shown earlier, studying the material world can lead us to God and help us know many things about Him. This error of the idealists helps atheists. If we cannot have any true knowledge of the material world, the proofs of God's existence go out the window.

➢ *An exaltation of the human mind, almost to the point of idolatry*. A century later, Enlightenment thinkers would talk about the "Goddess of Reason." We can see why people who so exalted the human mind would be quick to reject a God who is infinitely greater than any human intellect.

➢ *That human thought deals with ideas, not material objects*. Idealism maintains that what we are primarily aware of is ideas and representations, not the objects those ideas are supposed to represent.

➢ *Ideas treated almost as if they existed apart from the person who thinks them*. This is why this philosophy is called idealism.

➢ *External reality as we know it determined by our minds*. It is basically a projection of our own ideas. If material things have a reality of their own apart from our ideas, that reality can't be known, and so it's not important.

Comment: If the external world is whatever we think it is, what happens to our concept of God? He becomes only what we want Him to be. This means that when we worship our self-generated image of God, we are really worshiping ourselves. At this point, a person becomes an atheist for all practical purposes. In the next section, we will see how this idea that we create our own reality is very common in popular psychology and New Age religions.

This brief overview of idealism, the dominant philosophy of the 17th century, helps us understand how it paved the way for later atheistic philosophies.

PANTHEISM

The word "pantheism" means "God everywhere." Pantheism can take many forms. But in general, pantheism believes that God and the universe are the same.  God is not *distinct* from the world; God *is* the world. In this view, God is not a person but merely the natural "force" or forces that sustain and shape the universe.

Pantheism believes God and the universe are the same.
God is not distinct from the world;
*God **is** the world.*

As Christians, we believe that God is indeed present everywhere through His power, knowledge, and essence. However, He is distinct from His creation and transcends (stands outside) it. Since He reasons and wills, God is very much a person. In fact, He is three persons.

Pantheism can be found in ancient religions, especially Hinduism. It was revived in Europe by the modern philosophers **Giordano Bruno** (1548–1600) and **Baruch de Spinoza** (1632–1677). Spinoza was an influential philosopher. His pantheistic beliefs caused many well-known modern philosophers to adopt similar views.

Giordano Bruno

Pantheism can lead to atheism: if God is identical with the world, then He has no will, no authority, and no commandments. He teaches nothing and demands nothing. This notion of God is so watered-down as to be virtually meaningless.

Baruch de Spinoz

FIDEISM

Fideism was common among many early Protestants and among some of the most famous Christian idealist philosophers, such as **Immanuel Kant** (1724–1804). Fideists hold that we cannot know anything about God and spiritual realities through reason. We must have "blind faith."

Immanuel Kant

At first glance, fideism can appear to be a praiseworthy, biblical faith. However, it is a serious error that helped pave the way for atheism. Fideism falsely sets faith in opposition to reason, or it sees no place for reason in matters of faith.

Reason, rightly used, removes obstacles to faith and helps us understand it more deeply. Reason also enables us to explain and defend our faith to others. Faith divorced from reason easily becomes stagnant and sterile. This kind of faith is unimportant in the world, considered at best *irrational*, at worst *superstitious*.

Fideism holds that we cannot know anything about God and spiritual realities through reason. We must have "blind faith."

The notion of "blind faith" prompted many people who valued reason to become atheists. Moreover, by discrediting reason, fideism crippled Christianity's ability to respond to the intellectual attacks of the Enlightenment.

In his encyclical *Faith and Reason*, John Paul II points out that growth in our Christian faith requires both faith and reason. He emphasizes that since both are gifts from God, faith and reason must never be pitted against each other. Faith enables reason to accept what it cannot fully understand. Reason in turn enables us to understand our faith better and defend it against error.

EMPIRICISM

Empiricism was popular in Britain from the 16th through the 18th centuries. Along with idealism, which was dominant in continental Europe, empiricism strongly influenced the Enlightenment movement.

Empiricism was in some ways a reaction against the extreme rationalism of idealism. Recall that idealism emphasized *reason* as the source of knowledge, downplaying the role of the senses. In contrast, the empiricists tended to emphasize the role of the *senses* in acquiring knowledge, being skeptical of reason as a reliable source.

> *Empiricism emphasizes*
> sensible experience *rather than*
> abstract reasoning.
> *It tends to care more about what*
> *is practical and useful than in*
> *what is true or right.*

Empiricists were generally more concerned with acquiring practical information than in pursing ultimate truths. Their concern was not "is it true or right?" but rather "does it work and is it useful?" Empiricism quickly evolved into pragmatism and utilitarianism. Empiricists focused especially on political matters. They had an exalted and purely secular view of the state. Empiricists tended to ignore God rather than deny or oppose Him. Some influential empiricists were Francis Bacon, Thomas Hobbes, and John Locke.

Even in this brief overview, we can readily see the profound influence empiricism had in the evolution of the many modern atheistic systems.

Francis Bacon (1561–1626)

Thomas Hobbes (1588–1679)

John Locke (1632–1704)

THE ENLIGHTENMENT

The Enlightenment was an intellectual movement that swept through Europe in the 18th century. It radically transformed Europe and, ultimately, the modern world. The Enlightenment was concentrated mainly in France. However, since France was the cultural center of Europe, French ideas and movements quickly spread to the rest of the continent and beyond.

The Enlightenment was an 18th-century intellectual movement that rejected traditional religious beliefs and stressed the primacy of reason and the strict scientific method.

The Enlightenment was a comprehensive, well-organized, and brilliantly led movement to eliminate Christianity from modern society. It began with Deism as its religious creed, but eventually rejected all transcendent notions of God. It finally became a religion of "human progress" and the "Goddess of Reason."

Although the Enlightenment is often called a philosophical movement, it was really a radical revolution against Christianity and the established political and social order of 18th-century Europe. It is true that the leaders of the Enlightenment called themselves philosophers. But they weren't serious thinkers in the area of philosophy. They simply took the philosophical ideas of the previous century and adapted them for their anti-Christian crusade.

Denis Diderot

The best known leaders of the Enlightenment were such men as Denis Diderot, Voltaire, and Jean Jacques Rousseau. Many were extremely gifted writers and propagandists. Voltaire, for example, was the most famous writer in 18th-century France. Their most important accomplishment was putting together a thirty-five-volume work called the

Voltaire

Encyclopedia, compiled between 1750 and 1780. The writers claimed that these

Jean Jacques Rousseau

books contained all the knowledge then available in literature and science. In reality, these books used science and literature to cleverly promote Enlightenment ideas.

The *Encyclopedia* was enormously successful, quickly spreading the ideas of the Enlightenment throughout France and Europe. By the end of the 18th century, the intellectual revolution was complete.

The following is a brief summary of the main Enlightenment ideas:

➤ A radical *anti-Christian sentiment* that eventually became atheistic.

➢ A pagan, *hedonistic morality*.

➢ The concept of a *thoroughly secular state*. Enlightenment writers wanted to totally remove religion from all aspects of civil government. They had such an exalted view of this new secular state that it became a substitute for God. Some even spoke of the state as if it were divine.

➢ A complete *disregard for past history and traditional institutions*. Adherents despised the Church, monarchical governments, and all traditional authorities. They had nothing but contempt for the learning and culture they inherited from past generations.

➢ A naïve idea that science would inevitably lead to *unending human progress*.

➢ A *radical egalitarianism*. They were hostile to the nobility, the upper classes, and traditional privileges and ranks.

➢ An *unlimited view of freedom*. They believed that people do best when they are free of all restraints.

➢ An extreme *rationalism*. The French philosopher **René Descartes** (1596–1650)

René Descartes

is the father of modern rationalism. Rationalists believe that the only certain source of truth is human reason. However, Descartes was also a Christian. So he simply put a wall between his philosophy and his faith; he believed with "blind faith." He failed to see his error. Descartes certainly didn't realize that later generations would take his philosophy and use it as a substitute for faith. The Enlightenment leaders replaced faith with the philosophy of atheistic rationalism. They even spoke of the "Goddess of Reason."

Through their *Encyclopedia*, Enlightenment thinkers achieved an intellectual revolution. This set the stage for a bloody, physical revolution. The French Revolution, one of the most savage rebellions in history, began in 1789. Its purpose was to overthrow the governments of Europe and replace them with "revolutionary" administrations that would implement the ideas of the Enlightenment, by force if necessary. The Enlightenment architects were successful beyond their dreams.

In 1799, **Napoleon Bonaparte**

Napoleon Bonaparte

(1769–1821) became dictator of France. Not only a masterful military leader, Napoleon was also a true son of the Enlightenment. In a few years, he conquered much of Europe. Wherever he took control, he quickly put people in charge who would implement the ideas of the Enlightenment. Napoleon's domination of Europe ended in 1815, with his defeat at Waterloo.

By that time, however, Enlightenment ideas were deeply entrenched throughout Europe. They would continue to permeate Europe and the rest of the world for the remainder of the modern age. They would give birth to the many atheistic systems that have plagued the world in the last two centuries and have caused so much bloodshed and savagery. In the next section, we will examine some of the most important atheistic systems spawned by the Enlightenment.

ATHEISTIC SYSTEMS OF THE 21ST CENTURY

We will now look at the major atheistic systems of the present. In no other period of human history has atheism flourished as it has now. Although current atheism has assumed many forms, they can all be traced to four major philosophies: *materialism, rationalism, scientism,* and *evolutionism.*

These philosophical systems overlap; most contemporary atheists draw on more than one. While many of the ideas of these four systems can be found in ancient philosophies, the Enlightenment shaped the forms these systems have now.

MATERIALISM

Materialists believe that the only reality is the material universe. They deny God, the spiritual soul, angels, and all other spiritual realities. Hard-core materialists deny universal ideas and free will, since these are spiritual realities. Materialism is the underlying philosophy of communism, which has enslaved billions since the early 1900s. Communists attempted to replace God with the communist state. They outlawed belief in God. In communism, atheists achieved their greatest victory.

> *Materialism maintains that the only reality is the material universe.*

We are creatures of sense. Our five senses put us in contact with the external world. Human knowledge, no matter how advanced, depends on knowledge that was initially obtained through the senses. Our contact with the material world through the senses is direct, concrete, and immediate. Our knowledge of spiritual realities requires that we reason with abstract concepts. This means forming immaterial ideas from the sensation of material things, a process that is obviously indirect, abstract, and less immediate. Because of this difference between knowing sensible things and spiritual things, many people accept the position of materialism: that the only reality is what can known through the senses and that spiritual knowledge is simply imaginary.

RATIONALISM

Atheistic rationalism has become popular in Western Europe and North America. Atheistic rationalists claim the only truths we can know with certainty are the truths gained through reason. They deny God, angels, spiritual souls, and anything supernatural. They say all these things are against reason and therefore not true.

> *Atheistic rationalism denies anything supernatural. It misuses the truth-finding power of reason to deny the ultimate truth—God.*

Because reason is a very reliable tool for arriving at truth, it is easy to see how people can be persuaded that the truths of the faith beyond reason, like the Trinity, are imaginary. In fact, atheistic rationalists deny the truths of the faith that *can* be known through the proper use of reason, such as the existence of God and the spirituality of the human soul. They misuse the truth-finding power of reason to deny the ultimate truth—God.

SCIENTISM

The Church has always promoted true science. The Church teaches that there can never be a conflict between the truths of science and the truths of faith. All truth comes from God, who cannot contradict Himself. In sound science, reason uses the tools of science to observe and measure the material universe. Authentic science gives us accurate information about the universe, but it is incapable of studying supernatural things. However, real science leads an open-minded scientist to God, the cause of the universe.

Scientism claims the only certain truths are those obtained through the scientific method.

The promoters of scientism say that the only certain truths are those obtained through the scientific method. They refuse to accept anything that cannot be observed, measured, or experimented upon. Scientism is a futile attempt by atheists to promote atheism through a misuse of science. Genuine scientists know the limitations of the scientific method. They know that science cannot disprove the existence of God or the supernatural because it can only study the natural world. Atheistic psychologists and neurologists who claim they have proved "scientifically" that there

is no spiritual soul have fallen into the error of scientism.

Modern science has made spectacular progress in unlocking the secrets of the universe and advancing technology. We can see how these successes might dupe unthinking people into accepting the errors of scientism. Amazing scientific achievements can blind the unwary to the limitations of the scientific method.

EVOLUTIONISM

There are many theories of evolution. As John Paul II noted, some of these theories can be compatible with Christianity. The one theory that the Holy Father confirmed is clearly *incompatible* with Christianity is the idea that the human race evolved from dead  matter through purely random processes. Evolutionism is an attempt by atheists to use the biological sciences to disprove the existence of God. It is a type of scientism. However, because of the great impact it has had in our time, we will devote a whole section to it.

Atheistic evolutionism claims there is no need for intelligent design to explain human life.

For many years, evolutionists have accumulated an impressive amount of biological evidence attempting to show how a higher type of animal could have evolved from a lower one. They claim that this supposed evolutionary chain can be completely explained by random biological processes, excluding the need for God. They claim this evolutionary process began when *nonliving* matter randomly came together to form the first "simple" living cell. This began the evolutionary life-chain; man is the latest product.

Over the years, atheistic evolutionists convinced many people that their theory was scientifically proven. They claimed to have shown that there is no need for intelligent design to explain human life. However, recent advances in molecular biology are contradicting the claims of atheistic evolutionists.[7]

Molecular biologists have shown that there is no "simple" living organism, no matter how small it may be. A living organism must be able to take in nutrition and chemically convert it to energy if it is to grow and multiply and form part of any evolutionary chain. For any living organism, no matter how primitive, to convert nutrition to energy requires biological systems that are unbelievably complicated. They are so complex that, even with all the incredible technology at our disposal, we are not even close to creating any living organism from nonliving matter. Yet atheistic evolutionists continue to insist that the first living organism was the result of chaotic processes in dead matter.

---

7 Readers interested in examining the biochemical details that undermine atheistic evolution should consult Michael J. Behe's impressive book, *Darwin's Black Box: The Biochemical Challenge to Evolution* (New York, NY: Simon & Schuster, 1996). See also the excellent DVD, *Unlocking the Mysteries of Life* (2002), which examines complex systems within the cell that point to intelligent design.

One of the greatest molecular biologists of our time and a hard-core evolutionist, **Francis Crick** (1916–), who with James Watson discovered the structure of DNA, has seen the writing on the wall. He recognizes the impossibility of dead matter forming a living organism through random processes. He now speculates that *aliens* planted the first living organisms on earth! At least he is acknowledging the need for intelligent design. Hopefully he will abandon fictional UFOs and turn instead to the true Intelligent Designer who has revealed Himself in so many clear ways.

Francis Crick

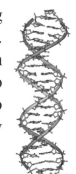

REFUTING ATHEISM

The arguments of materialism, rationalism, scientism, and evolutionism can appear convincing at first glance. Upon examination, however, we can refute all these atheistic systems by:

① Using the proofs we gave for the existence of God.

② Using the proofs we gave for the spirituality of the soul.

③ Using the evidence of the many scientifically documented miracles, especially those in recent times.

REFUTING THE NEW ATHEISTS

Atheists are on the attack. Richard Dawkins' *The God Delusion* (2006) and Christopher Hitchens' *God is Not Great* (2007) have become best-sellers.[8] Sometimes called the "New Atheists," these authors claim that belief in God is irrational and that religion is destructive.

How do we answer the New Atheists? We should note that the New Atheists are saying nothing new. They are simply re-warming the same objections that have been raised, and answered, for centuries. Many excellent books answer the particular claims of the New Atheists in detail.[9] But in general, we can answer atheists like Dawkins and Hitchens by showing how they misuse science and misrepresent Christianity.

ARE SCIENCE AND RELIGION AT WAR?

The New Atheists promote the idea that religion and science are at war. They claim faith and reason are fundamentally incompatible. This would certainly surprise leading scientists throughout history—including Copernicus, Kepler, Galileo, Descartes, Boyle, Newton, Pascal, Harvey, Faraday, Joule, Kelvin, Pasteur, Maxwell, Planck, and Mendel—all of whom were Christian.

The New Atheists depict Christians as ignorant, superstitious, and opposed to scientific inquiry. But it was Christianity that invented modern science and Christians who produced many of science's greatest achievements.[10] Modern science took root and flourished in a Christian culture that believed the order and rationality of the physical universe reflected the order and rationality of God. Christianity is not opposed to science, nor is faith opposed to reason. They work hand in hand.

Both atheists and believers see that the universe is orderly and rational. Both conduct scientific inquiry based on this truth. But while atheists take the order and rationality of the universe for granted, believers pursue the question of *why* the universe is this way. They conclude that the truths of the material world are not the product of chance, but of God who is the ultimate Truth.

Sir Isaac Newton (1643–1727), one of the greatest scientists in history, saw his discoveries as revealing God's intelligent design: "This most beautiful system of the sun, planets, and comets, could only proceed from the counsel and dominion of an intelligent and powerful Being."[11]

---

8 Also worth mentioning are *Letter to a Christian Nation* by Sam Harris and *Breaking the Spell: Religion as a Natural Phenomenon* by Daniel C. Dennett These four—Dawkins, Hitchens, Harris, and Dennett—are sometimes called the "four horsemen" of the New Atheism.

9 We especially recommend Dinesh D'Souza's *What's So Great About Christianity?* (Washington, DC: Regnery, 2007) and Thomas Crean, O.P.'s *God is No Delusion* (San Francisco: Ignatius Press, 2007).

10 See Thomas E. Woods, Jr.'s *How the Catholic Church Built Western Civilization* (Washington, DC: Regnery, 2005).

11 Sir Isaac Newton, *The Mathematical Principles of Natural Philosophy*, Book III.

22

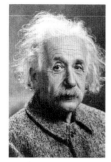

Albert Einstein (1879–1955), the greatest scientist of modern times, wrote that a conflict between religion and science "appears impossible":

Science can only be created by those who are thoroughly imbued with the aspiration toward truth and understanding. This source of feeling, however, springs from the sphere of religion. To this there also belongs the faith in the possibility that the regulations valid for the world of existence are rational, that is, comprehensible to reason. I cannot conceive of a genuine scientist without that profound faith. The situation may be expressed by an image: science without religion is lame, religion without science is blind.[12]

While he did not believe in a *personal* God, Einstein insisted he was not an atheist:

I'm not an atheist. I don't think I can call myself a pantheist. The problem involved is too vast for our limited minds. We are in the position of a little child entering a huge library filled with books in many languages. The child knows someone must have written those books. It does not know how. It does not understand the languages in which they are written. The child dimly suspects a mysterious order in the arrangement of the books but doesn't know what it is. That, it seems to me, is the attitude of even the most intelligent human being toward God. We see the universe marvelously arranged and obeying certain laws but only dimly understand these laws.[13]

"In view of such harmony in the cosmos which I, with my limited human mind, am able to recognize, there are yet people who say there is no God. But what really makes me angry is that they quote me for the support of such views."

—Einstein to Prince Hubertus of Löwenstein

Anthony Flew (1923–), for decades the most famous atheist in the world, recently changed his mind. Obeying the Socratic command to "follow the argument wherever it leads," Flew examined the significance of recent scientific discoveries—including the lawfulness of nature, the origin of life, and the Big-Bang—and concluded that a creator God must exist.[14]

Newton, Einstein, and Flew were unimpressed by the old arguments of the New Atheists. Also unimpressed are modern scientists like Francis Collins, Freeman Dyson, Paul Davies, John Polkinghorne, Max Planck, Werner Heisenberg, and Erwin Schrödinger, who reject the claim that faith and reason, or religion and science, are incompatible.

LIMITATIONS OF THE NEW ATHEISTS' WORLD VIEW

In place of God and religion, the New Atheists champion materialism, evolution, and science. But materialism, evolution, and science have considerable limitations.

---

11 Sir Isaac Newton, *The Mathematical Principles of Natural Philosophy*, Book III.

12 Nancy K. Frankenberry, *The Faith of Scientists: In Their Own Words* (Princeton, NJ: Princeton University Press, 2008), 161.

13 Frankenberry, 153.

14 Anthony Flew with Roy Varghese, *There is a God* (New York: HarperOne, 2007).

Limitations of Materialism

Materialism claims that physical matter is the only reality, and that everything in the universe—including thought, feeling, mind, and will—can be explained in terms of matter and products of matter.

If everything in the universe is matter or made from matter, then human thinking is a product of matter. Matter acts, not for its own purposes, but rather, out of necessity. Water doesn't *choose* to flow downhill; it simply must. But if all matter acts necessarily, following physical laws to inevitable results, then human thought—also a product of matter—is simply the result of necessary physical causes. Our thoughts, then, are not true or false. They simply *are*, as a necessary effect of our physical state.

If materialism is true, we are not *free* to choose one theory over another based on which fits the evidence better. We *must* think as we do, for all thought is the inevitable effect of physical causes. Therefore, it is absurd for us to try to "convince" another person that our idea is "true." Truth and choice are illusions. Atheists' attempts to persuade are sheer folly. No one can freely change his thinking, for a man's thoughts result from his physical condition. Of course, if his physical condition changes, then his thoughts will change correspondingly. But no one—including the atheist—is free to *weigh* the evidence, or *choose* the idea that best corresponds to reality. No one is free to think, let alone convert.

Materialism is self-contradictory. If materialism is true, then thoughts cannot be true—they simply are—including the thought of materialism. The claim that all thought is the necessary result of physical

G. K. Chesterton

conditions destroys the possibility of thought. It is, as G.K. Chesterton observed, a thought that stops all thought. If materialism is right, then thinking is an illusion, including thinking that materialism is right.

Materialism destroys the very things atheists extol: reason, free will, and ultimately, science. You can't do science if you can't form abstract, immaterial ideas. You can't do science if you aren't free to choose the theory that best fits the evidence.

Materialism grants atheists a victory, but at a terrible cost. Materialism does banish spiritual entities such as God. But it also eliminates abstract thought, freedom, and all human inquiry. Honest atheists will find this price too high.

Limitations of Evolution

As a scientific theory, evolution by natural selection has been extremely successful in explaining the genetic similarities between all living things. It can also account for the amazing diversity both within species and between species.

But evolution doesn't explain everything about life. It cannot, for example, explain the origin of life. Evolution can explain how living things transform, but it tells us nothing about how life started in the first place.[15] Evolution cannot explain human consciousness, our ability to perceive and understand the world around us. Nor can evolution explain human morality, our moral obligation to do what's right even when it's against our self-interest. Evolution is limited to biological changes, leaving untouched the more interesting questions about the origins of life, consciousness, and morality.

Furthermore, nothing in evolution is incompatible with belief in God.[16] Evolution could have been the mode by which God executed His design. He could have created directly or indirectly, instantly or slowly. He could have produced species by an external command or given them an interior power to change. Either way, God is still the ultimate cause.

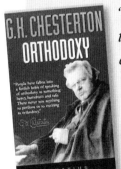

"If evolution simply means that a positive thing called an ape turned very slowly into a positive thing called a man, then it is stingless for the most orthodox; for a personal God might just as well do things slowly as quickly, especially if, like the Christian God, he were outside time."

—*G. K. Chesterton,* Orthodoxy

---

15 As more and more scientific discoveries contradict naturalistic explanations of the origin of life (see the DVD, *Unlocking the Mysteries of Life*, 2002), die-hard atheists will tend to follow either the Francis Crick path of science fiction and aliens or the Dawkins-Hitchens path of mud-slinging and misrepresentation.

16 A Catholic is free to investigate and embrace evolution as long he maintains: (1) the direct creation of the human soul (it is impossible for matter to create spirit); and (2) that the entire human race descended from Adam and Eve.

Limitations of Science

Science is the study and explanation of the physical world, based on observation and experimentation. Scientific discoveries and achievements have been astonishing.

But the tremendous successes of science shouldn't blind us to its limitations. By its nature, science only studies the observable universe. Science cannot study non-physical realities. Science has nothing to say about 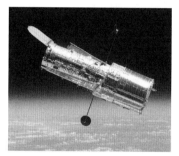 immaterial ideas (how long is the idea of justice? how much does it weigh?) or spiritual realities like angels, grace, or God. Science can't disprove spiritual or immaterial things because science only studies physical things. We cannot see God with either an electron microscope or the Hubble telescope. A good scientist knows what things are outside his field of study.

Science itself depends on non-scientific truths. Science cannot tell us *why* the universe is rational and accessible to the human mind. Science cannot tell us *why* the universe is consistent and obeys fixed laws. Only philosophy and theology can give us these answers. And yet the truth that the universe is rational and orderly is the foundation of all science. True science must avoid materialism, which destroys the possibility of reason and thus, science. The great power of scientific tools to discover truth shouldn't dazzle us into thinking they are the only tools to discover truth.

INTRODUCTION TO THE NEW AGE MOVEMENT

In the 1960s, many people in North America and Western Europe became attracted to Eastern religious ideas. In turn, these Eastern religions began to adapt their beliefs to better fit the Western mindset. Since many Americans and Western Europeans are extremely attached to psychology and modern science, the promoters of Eastern faiths began to express their religious ideas in psychological and scientific terms. Eventually, they even began to use Christian concepts to promote their teachings.

These adaptations were quite successful. By the end of the 1970s, Eastern beliefs had become popular throughout North America and Western Europe. This growing interest in adapted Eastern religions is often called the **New Age Movement** (NAM).

The Catholic Church is concerned about the immense inroads the NAM has made among Catholics. In 1989, the Vatican issued a document entitled *Some Aspects of Christian Meditation*, cautioning Catholics about the dangers of borrowing indiscriminately from Eastern meditation techniques.

John Paul II, in his book *Crossing the Threshold of Hope*, warns us that the NAM is in many ways a revival of Gnosticism: (NOS-ti-sizm), one of the most difficult heresies to plague the early Church.

In 1988, Archbishop Christopher Schönborn, O.P., editor of the *Catechism of the Catholic Church*, wrote a book entitled *From Death to Life— The Christian Journey*. In it, the archbishop expresses alarm that one-fourth of Christians in Europe believe in reincarnation because of the influence of the NAM. He spends one-fourth of his book explaining why reincarnation is totally incompatible with Christianity.

Polls taken in the United States indicate that one-fourth of Christians in *this* country also believe in reincarnation. Because of the great inroads made by the New Age Movement in Christian countries, the Vatican has addressed the NAM. In 2003,

the Pontifical Council for Culture and Interreligious Dialogue issued a document entitled *Jesus Christ, The Bearer of the Water of Life: A Christian Reflection on the "New Age."*

At first glance, the NAM appears to be a loose, fragmented, and unorganized collection of ideas. Upon further study, however, it becomes clear that New Agers hold several core beliefs, drawn from many identifiable sources. In the following sections, we will examine the main beliefs and sources of the NAM.

THE ROOTS OF THE NEW AGE MOVEMENT

GNOSTICISM

John Paul II points out in *Crossing the Threshold of Hope* that the NAM has many similarities to the ancient heresy of Gnosticism. Accordingly, we will give a brief summary of Gnosticism. As we proceed in the booklet, it will become clear just how much the NAM draws from this ancient heresy.

Ancient Gnosticism existed before the time of Christ. It was a multi-faceted and complex system. Instead of having its own clear hierarchy and institutions, Gnosticism simply attached itself to existing religions and blurred the distinctions between its beliefs and theirs. It would adopt the religious terms of the religion it had infiltrated, and gradually empty them of their traditional content. It would subtly reinterpret words and beliefs to give them a Gnostic meaning. Gnosticism was continually evolving and redefining itself in order to subvert the religions that were recurrently appearing in the ancient world.

All this made ancient Gnosticism difficult to combat. The NAM uses these same tactics to infiltrate established religions today.

When Christianity began to grow, the Gnostics worked to subvert it as they had other religions. Indeed, there is clear evidence that early Christianity had to combat Gnosticism even while the Apostles

Gnosticism is an eclectic, pre-Christian system offering salvation through secret knowledge (Greek: gnosis).

still lived. For example, in his letter to the Colossians, St. Paul warns them against those who follow "elemental spirits of the universe" (Col 2:8). St. John in his first letter warns against those who don't confess that "Jesus has come in the flesh" (1 John 4:2). Both warnings appear aimed at the early Gnostics who even then were infiltrating the Church.

In the second century, Christianity fought a life-and-death battle against Gnosticism. As foes, the Gnostics proved to be both stubborn and powerful. Because of their cunning tactics, they were extremely difficult to eradicate from the Church. Finally, St. Irenaeus, in his great masterpiece *Against Heresies* (written about AD 180–190), gave a detailed explanation of Gnosticism that

effectively exposed its errors. As we deal with this new version of Gnosticism and attempt to refute its beliefs, it is important to remember *Against Heresies*. In this thorough work, we will almost certainly find the answers we need.

Even though Gnosticism was constantly evolving, it could always be identified by several basic beliefs:

➤ The Gnostics believed in a "Divine Being" that was totally unknowable and unapproachable by ordinary people. This Divine Being radiated "junior gods"

(Aeons) which acted as a bridge between the Divine Being and the material world. One of these junior gods was called a Demiurge. This Demiurge created the material world. Although the Divine Being was unknowable to ordinary people, the Gnostics claimed to have secret knowledge ("gnosis") that enabled people to have contact with the Divine Being even while still in this world.

➤ The Demiurge made the material world evil. Thus, evil was not caused by the misuse of human freedom. Rather, evil is the inevitable result of our involvement with material things.

➤ Jesus was one of these junior gods. Because the material world was evil, the Gnostics rejected the Incarnation and the Real Presence of Christ in the Eucharist. Because matter was evil, they denied that Jesus, an "emanation" from the Divine Being, could assume a real material body.

➤ Since the Gnostics believed all material things were evil, they disdained the body. They considered the spiritual soul to be the only good part of a person. The soul was chained and imprisoned by the body. They offered people "liberation" from the body through Gnostic beliefs and practices.

➤ They believed that the teachings of Jesus written down in the New Testament were for the "uninitiated" masses. These teachings were incapable of bringing salvation, as they understood the term. They claimed Jesus gave secret oral doctrines to His disciples that were meant to be passed on privately to the "enlightened" few.

➤ For the Gnostics, salvation meant becoming enlightened by learning the "hidden secrets" of Jesus. Thus, salvation depended not on grace but on acquiring a special knowledge. Sin was not a moral evil, but ignorance of the hidden knowledge possessed only by enlightened Gnostics.

EASTERN RELIGIONS

Although the NAM draws its religious beliefs from many sources, it derives the core of its spirituality from Eastern religions, primarily Hinduism and Buddhism.

The foundation of the NAM is **Hindu Pantheism**. This is the belief that everything is One (Brahman), and the One is God.  The world as we know it is an illusion. We think we see separate things, individual people, and contrasts like good and evil. This is all an illusion (Maya). The goal in this life is to discover the oneness and divinity of all things. We are to discover the divinity within us; we must realize that *we* are God!

Hindu Pantheism believes that everything is really One thing, and the One Thing is God. It highlights the oneness and divinity of all things.

This discovery that we are God brings with it the recognition that all is one. We lose our individual personalities and become absorbed into the One. Being absorbed into the One is called Nirvana. The One is not personal. It is best described as the "Universal Energy" or "Universal Force."

How do we achieve this absorption into the One? Ordinarily, it takes thousands of reincarnations to attain a "higher consciousness" that enables us to recognize the divinity and oneness of everything. Luckily, there is a short cut to Nirvana. We can learn the secret wisdom of the "Ascended Masters" or "Avatars." These are beings who have attained Nirvana, but are allowed to make contact with this world in order to teach us how to shorten the reincarnation process through a special "enlightenment."

Nirvana is recognizing that all things are one and being absorbed into the One.

Sculpture of a Hindu Yogi

Hindu masters called Yogis or Gurus have this knowledge and can teach it to us. Learning this way of enlightenment involves Eastern meditation and special postures (yoga). The NAM considers Jesus to be an Ascended Master or Avatar. Remember, the Ascended Masters have no personalities. They temporarily assume these in order to communicate with us.

Even in this brief review of Eastern religious beliefs we can see Gnostic similarities. The Eastern concepts of the One, the Ascended Masters, the special enlightenment, and Jesus as an Avatar resemble the Gnostic concepts of the unapproachable power, junior gods (Aeons), the secret knowledge or gnosis, and Jesus as an Aeon.

In the West, the most popular of all the Eastern beliefs is **reincarnation**. This is the view that a person's soul comes back to inhabit another body. The most extreme form of reincarnation teaches that we can return as a lower life form, such as a worm. However, most New Agers believe that we will reappear only in another human body.

Reincarnation is subject to Karma, the law of merit and demerit, gain and loss. If you do what is good, you gain positive Karma. If you do what is bad, you incur negative Karma. At the end of your life, your Karma is tallied up. If you end up with positive Karma, you will enter the next life closer to Nirvana. If you leave this world with negative Karma, you will enter the next body further from Nirvana. Moreover, in future reincarnations you will learn from experience why your bad acts were wrong. For example, if you beat your wife in this life, then in your next life you might be a battered wife.

Reincarnation is the view that a person's soul comes back to inhabit another body.

Those who accept reincarnation generally believe that it takes countless lives or incarnations to achieve Nirvana, the absorption into the One. This is why New Agers are so attracted to Gurus and Eastern meditation techniques which allow them to short-circuit the reincarnation process and enter Nirvana immediately.

MODERN PHILOSOPHY

Modern philosophy is another source for New Age thought. Modern philosophies took ancient beliefs like pantheism and explained them in philosophical and scientific terms. This gave them immense credibility among modern thinkers. They also interpreted ancient pagan ideas in new and creative ways. These adaptations made pagan beliefs appear novel and attractive to many modern people. Below are some of the more important ways modern philosophy influenced the NAM.

The Philosophy of Spinoza

Spinoza (see page 14) took ancient pantheism and gave it a systematic, philosophical foundation. Although the NAM's pantheism includes elements not found in Spinoza's, New Agers use Spinoza's teachings and philosophical arguments to lend credibility to their own beliefs.

Idealism

The NAM borrows the following ideas from idealism (see page 12):

➤ A negative view of the body. Idealists, like Gnostics, consider the body to be a burden for the mind. The NAM considers the body to be an obstacle to enlightenment, a temporary hindrance on the way to Nirvana where there will be no more bodies.

➤ Reality determined by our minds. An important idealist theme is that the external world is basically what our minds make it to be. This idea is fairly new; it's difficult to find prior to the modern age. The NAM embraced this notion and took it a step further: we can create our own unique reality! The NAM promotes this idea through books, movies, and mind-enhancing seminars. This radical form of escapism is very appealing to many people.

It also dovetails with the current infatuation with dreams.

➤ German Idealism (G. W. F. Hegel and others). The NAM borrows two important ideas from German Idealism:

① God is an impersonal Absolute; and

② evolution is the principle of all growth.

G.W.F. Hegel

Hegel's Absolute is virtually identical with the One of the NAM. New Agers constantly discuss their ideas in terms of evolution: everything is evolving, we are on the verge of an evolution to "higher consciousness," and Christianity is simply one phase of a spiritual evolutionary process. Christians obviously believe in growth and change. But Christians believe the principle of spiritual growth is grace, not some evolutionary dynamic.

MODERN PSYCHOLOGY

Modern psychology is a legitimate and useful discipline. Many disturbances of the mind are helped by good psychology. Our concern here is with a movement within modern psychology that departed from sound principles and ultimately became fertile soil for New Age beliefs. This movement is commonly known as the Human Potential Movement, which developed in the 1950s and reached its apex in the 1970s. Its central ideas eventually coincided with the key beliefs of the NAM.

First, we will look at some of the psychological beliefs found in the first half of the 20th century that were forerunners of the Human Potential Movement (HPM). Then, we will examine the HPM itself.

Carl Jung (1875–1961) had been a disciple of Sigmund Freud. Jung broke with his mentor because of Freud's contempt for all religious beliefs and his obsession with sexuality. Many believe Carl Jung to be one of the greatest modern psychologists. His impact on modern psychology is immense.

Although Jung, unlike Freud, recognized the value of religious beliefs, he drifted into Gnosticism and Eastern religions, becoming a pantheist. He believed religious beliefs should be based on personal experience, not objective truths. Jung is well known for his theory of the "collective unconscious"—that all the experiences of the human race are stored and passed on in a "consciousness" that belongs to everyone. Jung's religious beliefs affected his psychology. It isn't surprising that the NAM holds Jung in high esteem and refers to his teachings to support New Age beliefs.

Like Jung, **Wilhelm Reich** (1897–1957) is considered one of the greatest psychologists of the 20th century. He, too, had been a disciple of Freud. Reich taught that the universe is permeated by an "Orgone Energy." He said that psychological growth and wholeness depended on our connecting with this cosmic energy. Like Jung, Reich was also a pantheist. The NAM borrows from the works of Reich. The New Age "One"

and Reich's "Orgone Energy" are easily reconciled.

Sigmund Freud (1856–1939), the founder of modern psychology, had a very pessimistic view of humanity. Jung and Reich presented a more optimistic view of people and stressed the great potential of the human psyche. Unfortunately, their ideas became tainted with paganism. When the Human Potential Movement began in the 1950s, it drew heavily from psychologists like Jung and Reich. This explains why it quickly degenerated into pop religion.

THE HUMAN POTENTIAL MOVEMENT

Abraham Maslow (1908–1970) is regarded as the father of the Human Potential Movement. He set forth his ideas in his book *Motivation and Personality* (1954). Maslow thought that Freud had focused too much on the dark side of humanity. He saw more good than bad in people and held that human beings had great potential to grow in wholeness, goodness, and values. He taught that human beings, through their own powers, could become superhuman and God-like.

Maslow was an atheist, but he seemed to believe that human beings could essentially become divine by tapping into their hidden potentials. Maslow continually used expressions like "transcendence" and "self-actualization" to describe this unleashing of human potential.

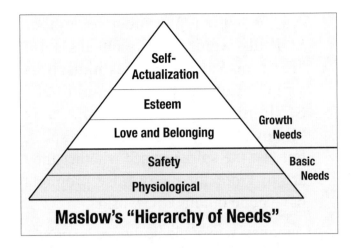

Maslow's "Hierarchy of Needs"

Maslow's teachings guided some of the most influential psychologists of recent times, including Erich Fromm, Rollo May, and Carl Rogers. They developed what became known as *humanistic psychology*. This became the dominant psychology taught in our colleges in the 1960s and 1970s. The two fundamental principles of humanistic psychology are that people are basically good and that they have unlimited potential for growth. Humanistic psychology asserts that, through psychotherapy, human beings can harness the unlimited potential they have within.

> *Humanist psychology asserts that people are basically good and have unlimited potential.*

Many people who were involved in the humanistic psychology movement became disappointed with it. They were dissatisfied with the results of humanistic psychotherapy; it didn't deliver "transcendence" and "self-actualization." Many weren't satisfied merely realizing their *human* potential. They wanted to be gods, and they wanted a better way to achieve divinity than psychotherapy.

This set the stage for the next development of the Human Potential Movement: Transpersonal Psychology. Developed in the late 1960s, Transpersonal Psychology promised a quick method for attaining divinity: Eastern meditation.

The first issue of the Journal of Transpersonal Psychology came out in 1969. It stated that Transpersonal Psychology was concerned with "ultimate human capacities." Among these capacities were cosmic awareness, unitive consciousness, oneness, and mystical experience. Transpersonal Psychology was thoroughly New Age from the beginning. Its ideas are identical to those found in New Age writings. The HPM had now become an instrument of the NAM.

How did the psychological movement concerned with developing human potential degenerate into New Age pop religion? First, it failed to recognize the pagan seeds planted by pioneers like Jung and Reich. Second, the HPM began delving into the spiritual, while ignoring sin, grace, and the true God. At this stage it simply became another pagan religion. It isn't surprising that it has become pantheistic in the end. C. S. Lewis astutely observed that all pagan religions tend toward pantheism. The only

checks against drifting into pantheism are belief in the true God and sound thinking. The HPM lacks both a belief in God and a valid philosophy.

C. S. Lewis

MISCELLANEOUS SOURCES

We have listed the major sources for New Age thought. However, like their Gnostic forerunners, New Agers are adept at latching onto popular movements and using them to promote New Age ideas. We will list just a few of these current movements and describe how they are being adapted by the NAM.

Angelic Apparitions

People are fascinated with angels. Many people are claiming to have seen angels, and some are writing books about their experiences. These accounts are often emotionally gripping. Because of this, Christians may overlook some of the disturbing contents of these alleged angelic

apparitions. For example, in one of the most popular books on angelic experiences, an "angel" reveals that there is no Trinity. In another popular book, the "angel" denies that there is a hell. Many of these angels identify themselves as "spirit guides" and "ascended masters." They are saying things that are clearly New Age, not Christian. Many Christians swallow New Age beliefs because these "angels" speak of past lives and the oneness of everything.

We must remember that what appears to be an angelic apparition can be one of four things:

① An authentic angelic apparition.

② A deception on the part of the seer.

③ The product of an overactive imagination (self-deception in this area is common).

④ An evil spirit. We must remember St. Paul's words in 2 Corinthians 11:14: "for even Satan disguises himself as an angel of light." We should heed St. John's warning in 1 John 4:1: "Beloved, do not believe every spirit, but test the spirits to see whether they are of God; for many false prophets have gone out into the world."

As Catholics, we should be guided by proper Church authority in this most difficult area of discerning spirits.

Near Death Experiences

In recent years, thousands of people have described near death experiences (NDEs). These occur when a person nearly dies (or is medically "dead" for a short time) but then revives. A person who has had a NDE often feels he has left his body. He seems to float about the room and has experiences beyond those found on earth, such as seeing dead relatives or encountering a light of unbelievable beauty. Often he feels great peace.

What are NDEs? May Christians believe in them? How does the NAM use them for its own purposes? NDEs are nothing

new. Those familiar with Plato's writings know that in the *Republic* (Book X, 614), he recounts a soldier's description of his NDE. This account, given over 2300 years ago, is similar to the thousands of NDE accounts we are seeing in modern times.

Although the Catholic Church hasn't issued a document on NDEs, we can safely make the following points. As Christians, we believe that we have a spiritual soul that can live apart from the body. We also know that in this world the body greatly restricts the movement and powers of the soul. It's quite reasonable to expect that in a NDE, the soul would begin to experience some of the unrestricted movement and powers it will have when completely separate from the body after death. (Of course, if the soul goes to hell or purgatory it will encounter restrictions of a new kind!)

From a doctrinal point of view, there is no problem with NDEs as we have described them above. The problem arises when people report experiences or teachings that are contrary to the faith. We would give the same precautions for reported NDEs as we did with reported angelic apparitions.

The NAM points to some similarities between what people claim to experience in NDEs and what New Agers claim we will experience when we attain "higher consciousness." For example, the NAM entices people with the claim that when you attain higher consciousness you will be able to travel through space (known as astral projection). They point to the freedom of movement by the souls in NDEs as evidence that astral projection is possible. They also claim that the great peace and illumination described in NDEs is just a foretaste of what awaits people who follow the NAM way to higher consciousness. We can readily see how people who have had NDEs or who are interested in them could be drawn into the NAM.

The Drug Culture

In the last few decades, millions of people have turned to drugs because of their mind-altering effects. Drugs like LSD are extremely powerful hallucinogens that cause people to experience bizarre distortions of reality. The effects of these drugs are often described as out-of-body adventures, mystical "highs," and a psychedelic blurring of fantasy and reality. People who have these experiences find it difficult to return to the mundane life of the real world. They crave deeper thrills and higher "highs."

The NAM finds fertile soil for converts among those who have been part of the drug culture. It promises the ultimate "high" through the path of New Age enlightenment. Not surprisingly, those involved in the drug culture tend to be receptive to the New Age message.

Although the NAM does not actively promote the taking of mind-altering drugs,  it is surprisingly tolerant of the practice. Marilyn Ferguson, considered one of the great pioneers of the NAM, writes in her book, *The Aquarian Conspiracy*:

It is impossible to overestimate the historic role of psychedelics as an entry point drawing people into other transformative technologies. For tens of thousands of "left-brained" engineers, chemists, psychologists, and medical students who never before understood their more spontaneous, imaginative right-brained brethren, the drugs were a pass to Xanadu [higher consciousness], especially in the 1960s.[17]

17 Marilyn Ferguson, *The Aquarian Conspiracy* (Los Angeles: J. P. Tarcher, Inc., 1980), 89.

Mind-altering drugs are introducing many people to the NAM.

The Entertainment Industry

It is impossible to exaggerate the role of entertainment in fashioning the beliefs and lifestyles of Americans. The entertainment media has become the dominant force in our culture. Countless leaders in the entertainment industry are New Agers. They promote their New Age beliefs through movies, television, and music. Some of the most popular songs of our time promote New Age themes (such as imagining no heaven or hell and remembering your divinity). Some of the most popular shows of our time make repeated references to "the force" (the New Age "One"), finding the light, or remembering past lives. When the entertainment industry portrays meditation, it is almost always *Eastern* meditation. It virtually ignores the rich tradition of Christian mediation.

The Occult

G. K. Chesterton observed that when people stop believing in the true God, the danger is not that they will believe in *nothing*, but that they will believe in *anything*. The void created by millions of people rejecting the true God has been filled by an explosion of interest in the occult.[18] Horoscopes, palm reading, ouija boards, tarot cards, crystal balls, and séances are everywhere. Millions of people will not begin their

day without consulting their horoscopes. Psychic hotlines abound. People crave to learn their own futures, communicate with the dead, and gain extra-sensory powers.

It is easy to see how millions of people fascinated by the occult would be easy prey for the NAM. Actress Shirley MacLaine is one of the most famous New Agers  in this country. Her books describing her conversion to the NAM have sold millions of copies. One of them, *Out on a Limb*, became a television series. Shirley MacLaine is remarkably candid about the role the occult played in her conversion. She began her journey to the NAM by dabbling in things like séances and reading books on the occult.

As long as people seek out the occult, the NAM will have a steady stream of converts. Since the occult will never satisfy the deep longings of the human soul, the NAM can always tempt these people with the ultimate mystery of "cosmic consciousness."

---

18 For more on the occult, see Father Frank Chacon's audio CD, "Reality of Devil Worship and Diabolical Attacks." To order, please see form at the end of this book.

REFUTING NEW AGE BELIEFS

The most effective tools for refuting New Age beliefs are sound reason and good philosophy. Sacred Scripture may be helpful with those New Agers who were previously Christian and still retain some respect for the Bible. In general, however, New Agers will either discount the Bible's authority or interpret it in New Age terms. For example, when we discuss Jesus with them, they will be thinking of *their* Jesus—a New Age avatar. To evangelize New Agers, we must be able to refute their foundational belief: Hindu Pantheism.

REFUTING HINDU PANTHEISM

The NAM believes that everything is one, and that everything is God. God is an impersonal force or energy pervading the universe. God and the universe are one. Human beings attain their final, eternal destiny when they leave behind their bodies and "dissolve" into the One. They lose their individual personalities, which were merely illusions, and become absorbed in the impersonal One. This view of God is false for the following reasons:

➤ We know from reason that the true God is all-powerful, all-knowing, all-present, unchanging, eternal, spirit, and one. By one, we mean that God is not composed of parts. We also know that the true God is uncaused, and that He is the cause of all created things—material and spiritual. These truths can be known through the five classical proofs of God's existence, which are simply the result of applying reason to the universe in search of ultimate or final causes.

➤ Because it is one with the material world, the pantheistic god must share in all the limitations of the material world. It obviously cannot be spiritual in its entirety. It must be *changing*, because change is necessarily part of the material world. Since the pantheistic god is subject to change, at any one time it is either acquiring what it didn't possess or losing what it once had. In either case, it is demonstrating its deficiency and imperfection.

➤ Moreover, since the pantheistic god is one with the material world, it must be *limited in space* and therefore not all-present. It must also be *composed of parts*, since matter is necessarily made up of parts. These are just a few of the difficulties of believing in a god that is one with the material world.

➤ New Agers believe that part of the world is spiritual, since they believe that the soul is spiritual. Therefore the One must be partially spiritual, since it includes everything. Yet the NAM teaches that the One is *not a person*. This is illogical. Contrary to NAM beliefs, spiritual substances cannot be impersonal. To be spirit is to be a person (to have reason and will).[19]

---

[19] To be matter is to be made up of parts and therefore to be impersonal. To be spirit is to lack parts and to have the faculties of reason and will. Therefore, spirit is always personal. All spiritual entities—whether God, angels, or souls—have reason and will; they are personal.

Human beings are persons precisely because they have a spiritual component: souls. To be a spiritual entity means to have spiritual faculties: intellect and will. If a entity can reason and love, it is a person! Therefore, the idea that the One is at least partially spiritual and yet not a person is simply impossible.

➤ Also, remember that spirits don't have parts. We can't add to them to make them larger nor subtract from them to make them smaller. Change like this is only possible with material objects that are composed of parts. A spirit's lack of parts is very significant. Because spirits have no parts to break up into, they are naturally indivisible and indestructible; they cannot be divided or destroyed. Therefore, the idea of a soul dissolving into the One is impossible. It is a mistake that results from treating spiritual substances as if they have material properties, which of course, they don't.

➤ New Age pantheism says that because all is one, there is no individuality, or opposites, or contrasts (such as good and evil), or true differences of any kind. Even the idea of a person is a hoax. In short, the entire world as we know it is an illusion. The idea that everything we see is a delusion is shocking to common sense. To accept it, we must deny the clear evidence of our senses. Moreover, we must completely discount the reliability of our reason. The NAM is promoting a religion of self-induced insanity, where neither senses nor reason can be trusted.

In everyday life, New Agers clearly see a difference between Hitler and

 Mother Teresa. They panic if they hear their loved ones were in an accident. They rush into a burning house if their child is inside. They get a lawyer if someone defrauds them. If New Agers truly believed everything is an illusion, they would do none of these things. Their lives totally contradict their professed beliefs.

➤ New Agers constantly say that they are the religion of love. Yet love cannot exist without persons. Love is manifestly a *relation* between persons. If the idea of person is an illusion, as the NAM claims, the idea of love becomes meaningless.

These are just a few of the many ways we can show New Agers that the logical consequences of their beliefs lead to results they themselves cannot accept.

Hindu pantheism cannot deal with causality:

① How did the material world, which is part of the One, come into existence?

② Who created human souls?

③ Are we to believe that the ultimate power or being is not even a person?

No impersonal substance (Brahman or One) can possibly be greater than a person, who has an intellect and will. Therefore the impersonal One cannot create persons since the creator cannot be less than its creatures.[20] Moreover, the desire to lose your identity and be annihilated in the cosmic soup of the One is repulsive to the normal mind.

With those New Agers who still respect the Bible, we can show them that from Genesis to Revelation God is constantly described as personal. He gives his name as "I AM WHO I AM" (Exodus 3:14). "I" is obviously a personal pronoun. St. John tells us that "God is love" (1 John 4:16). Only persons are capable of love. The Bible tells us that God is three persons: Father, Son, and Holy Spirit. These persons are not going to "absorb" us in heaven. They will give us the light of glory that will enable us to reach the perfection of our personalities and to have an eternal, loving relationship with the three persons of the Trinity. Ask New Agers to compare this Christian belief with their notion that they will abandon their personalities and be dissolved into the One.

There are many other ways to refute Hindu pantheism. But these arguments should be enough to convince a reasonable New Ager.

REFUTING REINCARNATION

As we mentioned before, the doctrine of reincarnation is closely linked to Hindu pantheism. There are several reasons why reincarnation cannot be true:

> *To evangelize New Agers, we must be able to refute their foundational belief: Hindu Pantheism.*

➤ It goes against reason. As the ancient Greeks came to realize, the soul isn't just "using" the body. A human being is a *union* of body and soul. The body is just as much a part of our person as the soul.

The soul is the life principle of the body and gives it its identity. Philosophers call the soul the *substantial form* of the body. A soul cannot inhabit different bodies; it is made to give identity to only one body.

Sound philosophy refutes reincarnation. We know that the molecules of the body are completely replaced every seven years or so. As the body grows, it changes dramatically. Sometimes bodies can be completely shriveled by disease, but then recover their former vigor. Through all these physical changes, the identity of the body remains the same because the soul continues to give it the same identity. After the resurrection, the body will be transformed, but the body's identity will not be changed because the soul's identity remains the same.

➤ Our soul makes possible our self-consciousness and our awareness of our own identity. If a man lives to be a hundred, he can still remember when he was a child. He is aware that he is the same person as he was then because his soul has not changed. If reincarnation were true, we should remember past lives and be aware that it was we who were living those lives. But people *don't* recall past lives like they remember their own childhood. Although there are more than six billion people in

---

20 An effect cannot be greater than its cause. The principle is simply this: we can't give what we don't have. For example, I can't give you $1000 if I don't have $1000. An impersonal creator could never have made personal creatures.

the world, New Agers can only point to a few dozen who supposedly remember former lives. This number is statistically insignificant. Furthermore, these few cases can be easily explained without resorting to reincarnation. If reincarnation were true, we should have billions of people giving unmistakable evidence of remembering previous lives.

➤ New Agers claim that we grow in  knowledge and become "enlightened" through many reincarnations. But how can this be if we can't recall our past lives? We can't learn from experiences we can't remember.

➤ Many New Agers believe that we can be reincarnated into lower life forms like dogs and cockroaches. This is wrong for at least two reasons. First, a human soul cannot be the life principle of a lower animal. Animals have their own kinds of non-spiritual souls. Second, if human souls could inhabit lower animals, these animals would display human intelligence, which they obviously don't.

➤ Reincarnation is supposed to be a process whereby people become "enlightened" through many lives. If this system were true, we should expect humanity to be steadily improving over time. However, humanity has been around for thousands of years and people are as wicked as ever. We obviously haven't learned from past lives.

➤ Why should we assume that people are going to learn from past lives? In a single life, we see many people growing more wicked with age. They are obviously not learning from experience. Why should it be any different if the process is stretched out over many lives? Like many ancient pagans, New Agers make the mistake of equating knowledge with virtue. Yet it is all too obvious that we can know what's right and still choose to do wrong. Increased knowledge doesn't necessarily lead to increased virtue. A thousand lifetimes might easily leave a person completely unchanged, or even a thousand times more wicked. If we observe human nature carefully and still cling to reincarnation, we should logically expect the mass of humanity to go through infinite reincarnations with no hope of ever reaching Nirvana (except for the lucky few who find a guru with the right connections!).

➤ For those New Agers who don't reject the Bible, we can point to passages like Hebrews 9:27 that indicate we die only *once*, and then face judgment:

> **Hebrews 9:27:** And just as it is appointed for men to die once, and after that comes judgment.

There are many other arguments that show reincarnation is false, but these reasons should be enough to demonstrate that this belief is contradictory and futile. We should encourage New Agers to study the Christian doctrine of the resurrection. They will see that it is far superior in every respect to the false doctrine of reincarnation.

CONCLUSION

The beliefs of the NAM are simply the worst of paganism disguised as a new religion. The NAM would like us to believe that it is the final evolution of religious development. However, the NAM merely promotes ideas that pagans themselves came to recognize as false.

The NAM imitates the tactics of the Gnostics. New Age proponents have no qualms about usurping any movement or trend to promote their beliefs. They are not above embracing even the occult and the drug culture, if these serve their purposes.

Lucas Cranach the Elder, *The Trinity*, undated, oil on wood panel, Museum der Bildenden Künste at Leipzig, Germany.

We can understand how pagans, who lacked public revelation, might have accepted beliefs like pantheism and reincarnation. But to see millions of people who have the benefit of Christian revelation falling back into these errors is tragic. Those who have abandoned the Christian doctrines of the Triune God and the resurrection for the New Age beliefs of pantheism and reincarnation remind us of the people described in:

> **2 Peter 2:20–22:** For if, after they have escaped the defilements of the world through the knowledge of our Lord and Saviour Jesus Christ, they are again entangled in them and overpowered, the last state has become worse for them than the first. For it would have been better for them never to have known the way of righteousness than after knowing it to turn back from the holy commandment delivered to them. It has happened to them according to the true proverb, The dog turns back to his own vomit, and the sow is washed only to wallow in the mire.

BEGINNING APOLOGETICS

SERIES

BEGINNING APOLOGETICS 1:
How to Explain & Defend the Catholic Faith
Father Frank Chacon & Jim Burnham

Gives clear, biblical answers to the most common questions Catholics get about their faith. *(40 pages)*   **$5.95**

STUDY GUIDE for Beginning Apologetics 1
Jim Burnham & Steve Wood

Guides the individual or group through 12 easy lessons. Provides discussion questions and extra material from the Bible, Catechism, and early Church Fathers. *(16 pages)*   **$4.95**

BEGINNING APOLOGETICS 2:
How to Answer Jehovah's Witnesses & Mormons
Father Frank Chacon & Jim Burnham

Targets these groups' major beliefs, and shows how to refute them using Scripture, history, and common sense. *(40 pages)*   **$5.95**

BEGINNING APOLOGETICS 2.5:
Yes! You Should Believe in the Trinity: How to Answer Jehovah's Witnesses
Father Frank Chacon & Jim Burnham

Refutes the JWs' attack on the Trinity and provides a clear, concise theology of the Trinity. *(24 pages)*   **$4.95**

BEGINNING APOLOGETICS 3:
How to Explain & Defend the Real Presence of Christ in the Eucharist
Father Frank Chacon & Jim Burnham

Proves the Real Presence using Scripture, early Church Fathers, and history. Gives practical ways to increase your knowledge and love of the Eucharist. *(40 pages)*   **$5.95**

BEGINNING APOLOGETICS 4:
How to Answer Atheists & New Agers
Father Frank Chacon & Jim Burnham

Traces the roots of atheism and the New Age movement. Refutes their beliefs using sound philosophy and common sense. *(40 pages)* **$5.95**

BEGINNING APOLOGETICS 5:
How to Answer Tough Moral Questions
Father Frank Chacon & Jim Burnham

Answers questions about abortion, contraception, euthanasia, cloning, and sexual ethics, using clear moral principles and the authoritative teachings of the Church. *(40 pages)*   **$5.95**

BEGINNING APOLOGETICS 6:
How to Explain and Defend Mary
Father Frank Chacon & Jim Burnham

Answers the most common questions about Mary. Demonstrates the biblical basis for our Marian beliefs and devotions. *(40 pages)*   **$5.95**

BEGINNING APOLOGETICS 7:
How to Read the Bible
Father Frank Chacon & Jim Burnham

Provides the basic tools to read and interpret the Bible correctly. Shows how to effectively refute the errors of some modern biblical scholars. *(40 pages)*   **$5.95**

BEGINNING APOLOGETICS 8:
The End Times
Father Frank Chacon & Jim Burnham

Explains what Catholics believe about the Second Coming, the Rapture, Heaven, Hell, Purgatory, and Indulgences. Refutes the errors of the "Left Behind" rapture crowd. *(40 pages)*   **$5.95**

BEGINNING APOLOGETICS 9:
How to Answer Muslims
Father Frank Chacon & Jim Burnham

Examines Islam's major beliefs, and shows how to refute them using Scripture, history, and common sense. *(40 pages)*   **$5.95**

CATHOLIC VERSE FINDER
Jim Burnham

Organizes over 500 verses showing the biblical basis for more than 50 Catholic doctrines – *all on one sheet of paper!* This amazing "Bible cheat sheet" helps answer the majority of non-Catholic objections. Fold it in half, put it in your Bible, and never be unprepared to discuss your faith again. *Printed on both sides, laminated.*   **$2.95**

BEGINNING APOLOGETICS SUPER SET
All 10 booklets, plus Study Guide & Verse Finder

The whole set for one low price!
$54.95